Full of Moonlight

Full of Moonlight

Haiku Society of America 2016
Members' Anthology

David Grayson

Editor

Haiku Society of America

New York

Full of Moonlight

Copyright © 2016 by Haiku Society of America
All rights revert to the authors and artist upon publication.

ISBN: 978-1-930172-15-9

Each poem in this anthology was chosen by the editor from a selection of published and unpublished haiku and senryu submitted by current members of the Haiku Society of America. Each participating member has one poem in the anthology.

Artwork/photography: Garry Gay

Book production: Mike Montreuil

Book cover design: Luminita Suse

Book layout: Lynda Wegner — www.freshimage.ca

Introduction

Acting as the editor of the 2016 Haiku Society of America anthology has been a tremendous undertaking. At times I felt like Issa's famous snail climbing Mount Fuji. But the process has also been rewarding in meaningful ways.

One chief reward is the insight it has afforded into the present state of American and English-language haiku. It's been delightful to live with the diversity (formal and topical) of English-language haiku: from nature-centered to intensely urban, from one-liners to the experimental.

The *shasei*, or nature sketch, is well represented. Michael Smeer's haiku is just one example:

circle by circle . . .
a finch hops through
last night's rain

For the North American reader, the *shasei* can offer a glimpse into nature's wonders beyond our borders, as the Australian poet Ron C. Moss shows:

dry billabong
the colours of moonlight
in the flame trees

The poets' creations included much memorable work about the relationship between people and the natural world (another classic focus of haiku). As someone who enjoys the outdoors, both of the following haiku rang true with my own personal experience:

hiking alone—
the sound of every
falling leaf

Sharon Hammer Baker

steep woody path—
pausing to watch
my breath catch up

Elizabeth Hazen

Beyond haiku grounded in the natural world, throughout this anthology the reader will also be treated to vignettes of daily life, the "bread and butter" material for haiku writers. Some of these poems are part of the longstanding humorous senryu tradition, such as:

that special spark
in the waitress' eyes
catch of the day

Olivier Schopfer

Comicon—
every Darth Vader
says he's my father

Susan Burch

Social and economic issues, prominent this past year, have also been addressed by our community. The poets have relied on key practices of the haiku craft: a focus on distinct scenes or images, and an approach of restraint and suggestion. The result is compelling and indelible work:

the homeless man
hammers his tent stakes deeper
cold snap

Joan Prefontaine

dusk-darkened river
migrant field workers
wash off the day

Ferris Gilli

Poems such as these are successful because they prompt empathy and leave the poem open for further interpretation. They are not heavy-handed or pedantic, attributes that can close a poem and put off the reader.

Even when politics are directly addressed, the poets did so by emphasizing the subjective experience of the political process rather than rhetorically promoting or condemning a particular candidate or issue. The benefit of this approach is that a poem remains relevant beyond the current election cycle.

latest poll
the butterfly
almost within reach

Perry L. Powell

election year
not knowing what to make
of the sky

Michael Henry Lee

In addition to the variety of subject matter, I was
also impressed by the stylistic and formal qualities
in the submitted work, including rich imagery. To
use an unconventional example, there were several
poems about whiskey—offering vivid literal and
figurative images:

whiskey
in a coffee cup
my arm around the moon

Ken Olson

long summer
the whiskey glass full
of midnights

Tom Drescher

A breadth of forms was in evidence as well. Besides
the prevalent three-line and one-line forms, there
were outstanding two-liners. The following haiku
work best in two lines, and could not be improved
upon with another format.

worn magazines
—the waiting

Denise Fontaine-Pincince

evening on the lake—
oars dip into their own silence

David Rachlin

Interesting but unconventional work includes this whimsical example from Lew Watts:

haiku ~~group~~ workshop—
~~our~~ silly smiles queue~~ing~~ up
to ~~share~~ scuttlebutt

Another pleasure of editing has been immersing myself in the poetry. A whopping 378 entries were submitted from nineteen countries. In choosing poems for inclusion, I didn't employ a strict process or algorithm. When there were equally strong haiku in a single submission, in some cases I preferred an unpublished one—eager to share with readers. In others, I chose a published gem. Sometimes the whole collection informed my choice—for instance, if there was an option to choose a poem that was stylistically or topically unusual.

Regarding the ordering, I experimented with a few schemas. Ultimately I succumbed to the serendipity of alphabetization, which hopefully will reward readers with surprises I could not have otherwise engineered.

I thank Fay Aoyagi for inviting me to act as editor; Garry Gay for the use of his fantastic photography; and Mike Montreuil for assistance with the book production. Thanks also to all of the members who contributed to this annual milestone. Through correspondence, I've gained a better understanding of the value of the Haiku Society of America's anthology to our members. I hope my effort has done justice to this importance.

On a final note, the title of the collection is inspired by a poem from Christopher Herold:

no more wishes
all the dandelion globes
full of moonlight

As the work on *Full of Moonlight* comes to a close, I feel a sense of satisfaction not only from its completion but also in reading the finished product: the delightful haiku and senryu from members around the world. I hope that readers will feel the same.

David Grayson
Editor

first snow
paper snowflake cuttings
dust our wood floors

Meredith Ackroyd
Afton, Virginia

secrets well kept
cloud shadows cross
the mountains

Mary Frederick Ahearn
Pottstown, Pennsylvania

a cored apple—
unable to laugh
or cry

Mimi Ahern
San Jose, California

spring feeding
the small black bird's joy
is my moment

Francis W. Alexander
Sandusky, Ohio

as I come to terms
the scent of approaching rain
resting on the sill

Phil Allen
Hartland, Wisconsin

Sudden gust of wind
kite caught in tree
tangled relationship

Catherine Altimari
Powder Springs, Georgia

crossing the bridge where he jumped the city lights

frances angela
London, England

a light snowfall without forming opinions

Susan Antolin
Walnut Creek, California

hazy moon
an H-1 visa
issued to the fox

Fay Aoyagi
San Francisco, California

daydreaming
the taste of coffee lingers
in church

Adam T. Arn
Belgium, Wisconsin

yellow tulips—the smell of splashing water

Eric Arthen
Worthington, Massachusetts

tropical storm
moving east on a snail's back
one raindrop per inch

Marilyn Ashbaugh
Edwardsburg, Michigan

cemetery elms, in the quiet they create for silent prayers

Francis Attard
Marsa, Malta

a ripple widens forgetting his face

Susan B. Auld
Arlington Heights, Illinois

hiking alone—
the sound of every
falling leaf

Sharon Hammer Baker
Findlay, Ohio

12

dead heading
tiny seeds cling to me
forget-me-nots

Shelley Baker-Gard
Portland, Oregon

family album . . .
lights of a passing train
in the night

Ludmila Balabanova
Sofia, Bulgaria

summer sky
curve and dip
of swallows

Mary Jo Balistreri
Genesee Depot, Wisconsin

estate sale
the cat circles
on the old chair pad

Caroline Giles Banks
Minneapolis, Minnesota

dandelion down to the bare necessities

Francine Banwarth
Dubuque, Iowa

ripening plums
the patience I never quite
got the hang of

Johnny Baranski
Vancouver, Washington

Iaido class
learning seated kata
beneath the hands of the clock

Sheila K. Barksdale
Bishops Cleeve, Gloucestershire, United Kingdom

breakfast on a verandah—
whatever we had
the blackbirds wanted

Janelle Barrera
Key West, Florida

fireflies briefly Ursa Major

Stuart Bartow
Salem, New York

Walking toward
A crooked smile
December moon

Mike Barzacchini
East Dundee, Illinois

tucked under
a cottonwood bough
the space station

Gretchen Graft Batz
Elsah, Illinois

back to the bluffs
of my childhood
1 Mississippi . . .

Donna Bauerly
Dubuque, Iowa

bicurious the moon within the moon

Roberta Beary
Bethesda, Maryland

crowding clouds layer
on layer rain
through falling leaves

R. Michael Beatty
South Bend, Indiana

girlfriends
forty-year reunion
depth of laugh lines

Lori Becherer
Millstadt, Illinois

memorial service . . .
a brown banana
turns the rest

Sidney Bending
Victoria, British Columbia, Canada

solitude . . .
the rock one sees
when the water's low

Brad Bennett
Arlington, Massachusetts

night wind
a skateboard rattles by
without a rider

Ernest J. Berry
Blenheim, New Zealand

late May on the playground
children leapfrog
into summer

Peggy Hale Bilbro
Huntsville, Alabama

spring breeze
the sailboat
pixelated

Robyn Hood Black
Beaufort, South Carolina

just hens in the rain without a verb

Meik Blöttenberger
Hanover, Pennsylvania

lightning—
a fly's wing flutters
    off the web

        brett brady
        Pahoa, Hawaii

    moonrise
    still out there weeding
    in her sunhat

        – Doris Kramer, 1928-2004

        Chuck Brickley
        Daly City, California

retirement day the veraison of me

    Alan S. Bridges
    Littleton, Massachusetts

the hollow space
around the apricot pit . . .
summer's end

Marjorie Buettner
Chisago City, Minnesota

Comicon—
every Darth Vader
says he's my father

Susan Burch
Hagerstown, Maryland

in the mirror
an old woman
has taken my place

Merle Burgess
Yorktown, Virginia

swallowtail
flies aslant
september dusk

Alanna C. Burke
Santa Fe, New Mexico

house fly
trapped behind the screen
summer moon

Norma Jean Byrkett
Preston, Washington

her quick hands garden,
      play music on pole-bean strings,
            loosen what's tethered

Cathy Cain
Lake Oswego, Oregon

writing down my dream
at daybreak
birds chattering

Cherry Campbell
La Mesa, California

heat wave
the corn's shadow moves
half an inch

Pris Campbell
Lake Worth, Florida

cold twilight—
the owl's gaze
unseen

Theresa A. Cancro
Wilmington, Delaware

full moon
pine tree shadows
sway on adobe wall

John J. Candelaria
Corrales, New Mexico

white wing
of the crescent moon
herons fledge

Matthew Caretti
Seo-un Hermitage, Gyeongnam Province,
Republic of Korea

lonely winter
a telephone wire
connects the stars

Sean Carlton
Long Beach, California

starlit sky
laced through redwoods
our reunion

Eleanor Carolan
Felton, California

missing women
the cold light
of an abalone moon

Terry Ann Carter
Victoria, British Columbia, Canada

plant sale raising food for the animal shelter

Thomas Chockley
Plainfield, Illinois

simplicity
of a single cherry tree
petals on the lake

Margaret Chula
Portland, Oregon

know thyself—
the bottom sides of the leaves
pale by contrast

Rick Clark
Seattle, Washington

back road
at least a thousand acres
of clouds

Tom Clausen
Ithaca, New York

Spanish moss
always that tangle
skyward

Lesley Clinton
Sugar Land, Texas

a wrist too thin
for father's watch
deer trail

Glenn G. Coats
Prospect, Virginia

prairie road—
raindrops
star the summer dust

Lysa Collins
White Rock, British Columbia, Canada

last parking space
a robin splashing
in the puddle

Sue Colpitts
Peterborough, Ontario, Canada

wings of the luna moth
closing   closing
hospice night

Ellen Compton
Washington, DC

the rattle
of a space heater
office politics

Susan Constable
Parksville, British Columbia, Canada

a jumble of stars
till i find orion—
a mathematician's elegant proof

Wanda Cook
Hadley, Massachusetts

Milky Way . . .
what it means
to mean the world

Amelia Cotter
Chicago, Illinois

everywhere
the scent of green
after rain

Dina E. Cox
Unionville, Ontario, Canada

military cemetery the formations of tulips

Kyle D. Craig
Indianapolis, Indiana

winter morning
lube beside the bed

Daniel Shank Cruz
Utica, New York

curled up
with a scratchy LP
Valentine's Day

Dan Curtis
Victoria, British Columbia, Canada

30

red purple
break the soil
peonies

John-Carl Davis
West Bend, Wisconsin

tree
a life encoded
in rings

Pat Davis
Pembroke, New Hampshire

summer sunset smokes on the fire escape

Bill Deegan
Mahwah, New Jersey

great egret flies
wings touching the tips
of his reflection

Marcyn Del Clements
Claremont, California

my body
out of a million mothers—
budding leaves

Kristen Deming
Bethesda, Maryland

seed on the driveway
flashes of bright blue
indigo buntings

Brian DeMuth
Bowie, Maryland

wind-ruffled lake—
ducks curl into themselves
in autumn light

Angelee Deodhar
Chandigarh, UT, India

"Season's Greetings" . . .
braggart's annual letter
fuels the yule log

Charlotte Digregorio
Winnetka, Illinois

boy walking dog walking boy

Connie Donleycott
Bremerton, Washington

( )
my life
without her

Thomas Dougherty
Freedom, Pennsylvania

long summer
the whiskey glass full
of midnights

Tom Drescher
Rossland, British Columbia, Canada

arrivals gate
all faces the same
until yours

Anna Eklund-Cheong
Croissy-sur-Seine, France

early sunbright
cobalt and cold degrees
snowfallglitter

Art Elser
Denver, Colorado

oh, the humanity!
"Love Me Tender"
on a tuba

Haiku Elvis
Shreveport, Louisiana

Geese circling the sky
on rising tides of wind
Wings tilted towards home

Scott Endsley
Concord, California

From my roof
I could leap into that tree
and disappear

Bruce England
Santa Clara, California

burned down
my psychic barn revealing
the psychic moon

Robert Epstein
El Cerrito, California

white wedding
the brides kiss

Robert Ertman
Annapolis, Maryland

swishing ... scorpions burrow in snippets of curly tail shadows

Frances Farrell
Coon Rapids, Minnesota

low tide
from a much older ocean
fossil clams

Ignatius Fay
Sudbury, Ontario, Canada

the gate latched
I drop deeper
into the canyon

Bruce H. Feingold
Berkeley, California

down the first
and third base lines
cherry blossoms

Michael Fessler
Sagamihara, Kanagawa, Japan

from the bluebells
a bee zigzags around
I buzz off

Diarmuid Fitzgerald
Dublin, Ireland

aspen leaves
trapped in the eddy
our tête-à-têtes

Marilyn Fleming
Pewaukee, Wisconsin

worn magazines
—the waiting

Denise Fontaine-Pincince
Belchertown, Massachusetts

Evening chill
the sound of the wind
on its way to the sea

Sylvia Forges-Ryan
North Haven, Connecticut

her voice cracks   dogwood petals   drifting downstream

Mark Forrester
Hyattsville, Maryland

39

tea ceremony—
it starts & ends
with an empty cup

Stanford M. Forrester
Windsor, Connecticut

July 4th traffic
the road they took
to Gettysburg

Robert Forsythe
Annandale, Virginia

harvest moon
gulls sleeping
without heads

Tom Lyon Freeland
Edmonton, Alberta, Canada

winter rain . . .
the burning bush
leafs out

Ida Freilinger
Bellevue, Washington

heat index—
again you tell me
how I feel

Terri L. French
Huntsville, Alabama

outside the Salvation Army
a man wearing
my winter coat

Jay Friedenberg
New York, New York

Miss America photos
stare at the backs of boozy old men
sitting at the bar

Susan Furst
Woodbridge, Virginia

peepers early
waning moon
hangs in the maple

Marilyn Gabel
Agawam, Massachusetts

Memorial Day . . .
beside cross, crescent and star
. . . same flag

William Scott Galasso
Laguna Woods, California

labyrinth
a snail
cuts across

Dianne Garcia
Seattle, Washington

in my pocket seeds of another summer

Tim Gardiner
Manningtree, Essex, England

old lover
brings a bottle of wine
quicksand

Marita Gargiulo
Hamden, Connecticut

gathering shells
in the ocean mist
foreign voices

Garry Gay
Santa Rosa, California

dusk-darkened river
migrant field workers
wash off the day

Ferris Gilli
Marietta, Georgia

just the scent
of the red beans' slow simmer . . .
winter evening

Robert Gilliland
Austin, Texas

afternoon sunlight
in the mail
your haiku

Joette Giorgis
Port St. Lucie, Florida

neighbor's travelogue
hearing it all again—
wild bergamot

Susan Godwin
Madison, Wisconsin

I build
my invisible wall
silence by silence

Mel Goldberg
Ajijic, Jalisco, Mexico

turning back time
clock on the mantelpiece
strikes VIII

Kevin Goldstein-Jackson
Poole, Dorset, England

wet morning . . .
one fairground ride
rotates

John Gonzalez
Ipswich, Suffolk, England

behind my eyes
versacolor tree frog's
arpeggios

Merrill Ann Gonzales
Dayville, Connecticut

cicadas
the rusty lock
still unlocks

Brent Goodman
Rhinelander, Wisconsin

afternoon viewing
the sunlight
dust clings to

LeRoy Gorman
Napanee, Ontario, Canada

one breath and my lungs
are frozen, I stand still
left to be eaten warm

Mimi Gorman
Ashford, Washington

guided by instinct
gliding the glades
anhinga

Carolyn Noah Graetz
New Orleans, Louisiana

mixing red and yellow paint
my son discovers
fire

David Grayson
Alameda, California

my third backing up accident
I can only go forward now

Mac Greene
Indianapolis, Indiana

winter beach walk
the herring gulls
at peace with me

Steven Greene
Haddon Township, New Jersey

grandma naps
next to her chair
an empty wine glass

Ronald Grognet
New Orleans, Louisiana

bottom of the hill—
a red tricycle
rusts into winter

Anita Curran Guenin
San Diego, California

dad's old friend
both gone now
all their stories

Maureen Lanagan Haggerty
Madison, New Jersey

home stretch
the dog adds an arm's length
to his leash

Autumn Noelle Hall
Green Mountain Falls, Colorado

migrating cranes
the shadows of evening
lengthen

John J. Han
Manchester, Missouri

February blizzard
an empty
birthday list

Bryan Hansel
Grand Marais, Minnesota

rain-slick road
past the beef processing plant
the lights burn all night

Tim Happel
Iowa City, Iowa

another night
her annoyance
at the moon

Patty Hardin
Long Beach, Washington

keeping me
from you
brake lights

Jon Hare
East Greenwich, Rhode Island

it's just the moon again
up to the same old same old
magic

William Hart
Montrose, California

so little left
of the no trespassing sign . . .
snowmelt

Michele L. Harvey
Hamilton, New York

haiku afternoon
the instructor's smile
feeling the chalk

Patricia Harvey
East Longmeadow, Massachusetts

full moon
skinny dipping
full moons

Arch Haslett
Toronto, Ontario, Canada

green tea . . .
time stays
in the cup

Tomoko Hata
Winnetka, Illinois

lazy days—
floating through the fog
of our breakup

Barbara Hay
Ponca City, Oklahoma

steep woody path—
pausing to watch
my breath catch up

Elizabeth Hazen
Williston, Vermont

another year
under my feet
maple leaves

Cynthia Henderson
Santa Fe, New Mexico

old pines
shoulder to shoulder
campfire ghosts

Randall Herman
Pilger, Nebraska

no more wishes
all the dandelion globes
full of moonlight

Christopher Herold
Port Townsend, Washington

farmers' market—
the different ways we say
tomato

Poppy Herrin
Gonzales, Louisiana

test results
a rainbow splices
the afternoon clouds

Merle D. Hinchee
Houma, Louisiana

walking backwards in the snow
the landmarks we chose
last summer

Carolyn M. Hinderliter
Phoenix, Arizona

city ants
in and out of
cement cracks

Judith Hishikawa
West Burke, Vermont

retirement cake—
eating myself
sick

Ruth Holzer
Herndon, Virginia

in one sound
the river passing
by

*Gary Hotham
Scaggsville, Maryland*

May moon—
a pair of cottontails dancing
in the dewy grass

*Elizabeth Howard
Arlington, Tennessee*

thistledown

a fossil trunk
forty-four million years old

Marshall Hryciuk
Toronto, Ontario, Canada

morning haze
Monet is painting
another garden

Marilyn Humbert
Sydney, New South Wales, Australia

fair leaving
the turbaned waxwork
still granting wishes

David Jacobs
London, United Kingdom

59

Bashō tosses bread
to the abandoned child
cold autumn wind

Eric Jennings
Atlanta, Georgia

old cemetery
snowflakes dissolve
before they land

Jeanne Jorgensen
Edmonton, Alberta, Canada

one thought over
laps another un
til both are gone

Jim Kacian
Winchester, Virginia

August sun . . .
when war was fought
with water guns

Elmedin Kadric
Helsingborg, Sweden

gunmetal the color of election year rain

Barbara Kaufmann
Massapequa Park, New York

snowflake clumps
fall silent through bare branches—
ghosts in forest

Robert K. Keim
Wolcott, New York

all around the campfire the dog's tongue

Julie Bloss Kelsey
Germantown, Maryland

middle of the night . . .
a train whistle
sings the blues

Mary Kendall
Chapel Hill, North Carolina

all in one day
snow to hail to rain to sun—
he's turning 13

Maggie Kennedy
Brookfield, Illinois

summer sea
a forgotten language
upwelling

Phillip Kennedy
Monterey, California

autumn hillside
a crow flies
as the crow flies

Bill Kenney
Whitestone, New York

my sister's grandson
lifts my heart when he calls me
Great Howard

Howard Lee Kilby
Hot Springs National Park, Arkansas

the question of children
a road sign announces
the Great Divide

Mary Kipps
Sterling, Virginia

getting dressed up
for the conference
call

kjmunro
Whitehorse, Yukon Territory, Canada

cherry blossoms
so near yet so far—
all my children

Marylouise Knight
Omaha, Nebraska

poets write
about poetry
nautilus shell

Tricia Knoll
Portland, Oregon

rain
showers
porch talk

Dianne Koch
Dubuque, Iowa

no note—
on the doorstep
garden tomatoes

Deb Koen
Rochester, New York

winter solitude
the company
of unshelved books

Deborah P Kolodji
Temple City, California

Cardinals
Birds of Pray

Ed Kosiewicz
Punta Gorda, Florida

spring training
ball players stretch
their winter escapades

S.M. Kozubek
Sarasota, Florida

red tulips
outside my dentist's window
open wider

Henry W. Kreuter
Lebanon, New Jersey

learning to talk
the hawk's
voice cracks

Steve Kuntz
Farmersburg, Indiana

ridge top
clouds float below
the sound of wind

Ron LaMarsh
Seattle, Washington

a watermelon moon
over deep snow—
the silence of crows

Jill Lange
Cleveland Heights, Ohio

becoming ronin
ant
on the car

David G. Lanoue
New Orleans, Louisiana

open window
a spring breeze blows in
children's laughter

Jim Laurila
Florence, Massachusetts

election year
not knowing what to make
of the sky

Michael Henry Lee
Saint Augustine, Florida

morning walk
taking on a new shape
algae in the pond

Phyllis Lee
Sebring, Ohio

first sign of spring
chalk pictures
on the sidewalk

Brenda Lempp
Madison, Wisconsin

catalpa tree
climbing into the clouds
of childhood

Antoinette Libro
St. Augustine, Florida

mosquito!
do you too
have a new granddaughter

Bruce Linton
Richmond, California

between I
& Orion
November winds

Joseph Llewellyn
Bristol, United Kingdom

forest fire—
believing I'll be
reborn

Cyndi Lloyd
Riverton, Utah

july wedding
not in the forecast
hail stones

Renee Londner
Prospect, Connecticut

I count
the ways I love her
IV drip

Gregory Longenecker
Pasadena, California

emergency room—
dried grapefruit halves
on the breakfast table

Amy Losak
Teaneck, New Jersey

steady rain
the pumpkin's
dark smile

Bob Lucky
Jubail, Eastern Province, Saudi Arabia

moon beams
split the forest night
still life

E. Luke
Rancho Palos Verdes, California

golden poppies
open to the sun—
Mother's Day

Janis Albright Lukstein
Rancho Palos Verdes, California

thought I knew
love's ins and outs
Double Dutch

Doris Lynch
Bloomington, Indiana

starry night
I wish on the one I imagine
her to be

Patricia J. Machmiller
San Jose, California

hot August night—
the dog's sigh
fills the darkness

Carole MacRury
Point Roberts, Washington

snow-covered pine
the hermit thrush sings
my song

Ann Magyar
Brighton, Massachusetts

unconcerned
with divorce rates
mating butterflies

Annette Makino
Arcata, California

74

campground quiet hours—
the conversation
of frogs

C.R. Manley
Bellevue, Washington

day of the dead
i find myself grieving
the living

Anna Maris
Övraby, Sweden

still
its spell
dried butterfly

Jeannie Martin
Arlington, Massachusetts

dustbin
still in full bloom
plastic roses

Thomas Martin
Beaverton, Oregon

holiday weekend . . .
three floors of modern art
I can't remember

Michael McClintock
Clovis, California

packing toddler's lunch
peanut butter sandwiches
shelled corn for the ducks

Wilma McCracken
Downers Grove, Illinois

barely autumn—
the sheet wrinkles
embossed on my thigh

Vicki McCullough
Vancouver, British Columbia, Canada

moon jellies
at the aquarium
all the screaming children

Tanya McDonald
Woodinville, Washington

church steps
an old man leaning
on the wind

Joe McKeon
Strongsville, Ohio

crinkling cellophane
how my baby brother laughed
eighty years ago

Dorothy McLaughlin
Somerset, New Jersey

antique shop—
in every mirror
an old face

Robert B. McNeill
Winchester, Virginia

watching your lips
curl
around those smart words

Connie R. Meester
West Des Moines, Iowa

Snow flakes
flying past headlights—
only whispers

Walter Mehring
Hanover, Pennsylvania

our houses ... our hills ...
what is the snow's name for snow?
for rivers? for spring?

Peter Meister
Huntsville, Alabama

snowy night
a single light traces
the far mountain road

RaNae Merrill
New York, New York

just the two of us
now in this house
the sound of rain

Ben Moeller-Gaa
St. Louis, Missouri

winter bones the body doesn't forget

Matthew Moffett
Mt. Pleasant, Michigan

all the progressive tenses in one memento mori

Beverly Acuff Momoi
Mountain View, California

days of snow
the congregation sings
of new beginnings

Mike Montreuil
Ottawa, Ontario, Canada

January clouds
she slices a purple onion
into halves

Lenard D. Moore
Raleigh, North Carolina

dry billabong
the colours of moonlight
in the flame trees

Ron C. Moss
Leslie Vale, Tasmania, Australia

October moon
everything
on this side or the other

Marsh Muirhead
Bemidji, Minnesota

moonrise
through winter trees—
her bulimia

Leanne Mumford
Sydney, New South Wales, Australia

my secret dream
warm wind moans
in the eaves

Marie Louise Munro
Tarzana, California

hot water//petals, leaves//tea blooms

Sandra J. Nantais
Crown Point, Indiana

November wind
the hollow places
that form a song

Peter Newton
Winchendon, Massachusetts

new snow—
the world outside my window
shrink-wrapped

Suzanne Niedzielska
Glastonbury, Connecticut

midnight
opening a window just enough
to let in the rain

Patti Niehoff
Cincinnati, Ohio

muddy garden boots
planting small puddles inside
eyes growing larger

Mike Nierste
Zionsville, Indiana

twilight
the young hooker
adjusts her skirt

Nika
Victoria, British Columbia, Canada

sighing of a breeze
the fragrant heather ripples
moving the mountain

Patricia Noeth
Iowa City, Iowa

evening walk
a heron tucked in
beside the pond

Nola Obee
Armstrong, British Columbia, Canada

in the holy well
the coins of the faithful
drop heavy with prayer

Frank O'Brien
West Bloomfield, Michigan

8 tips
into ∞
time ticks

> *Karen O'Leary*
> *West Fargo, North Dakota*

light falls
through yellow maple leaves
the mercy of God

> *Ellen Grace Olinger*
> *Oostburg, Wisconsin*

trapped in the
windshield wipers,
first leaves to fall

> *Bob Oliveira*
> *Bonita Springs, Florida*

whiskey
in a coffee cup
my arm around the moon

Ken Olson
Yakima, Washington

snow geese ascend
gathering dawn
into open wings

Marian Olson
Santa Fe, New Mexico

his latest revelation
bursts of frozen breath
dissolve in the wind

Mark Alan Osterhaus
Lake Mills, Wisconsin

sand dunes
by morning
a different dream

Renée Owen
Sebastopol, California

stale sermon inverts the preacher syntax his

Roland Packer
Hamilton, Ontario, Canada

deep space
her voice from the far side
of the bed

Tom Painting
Atlanta, Georgia

pushing the playground swings winter wind

Kathe L. Palka
Flemington, New Jersey

your thyroid surgery
the lump in my throat

Carol Ann Palomba
Wanaque, New Jersey

thought I'd seize the day
the day instead seized me
emergency room

Trilla Pando
Houston, Texas

leaning too far
out of the window—
the full moon

Sarah Paris
San Francisco, California

now just ten
letters define us—
cicadas burrow

Sarah Patterson
Arlington, Virginia

once again
flying dreams—
how can I stay

Thomas W. Paul
Newark, New York

mesquite smoke
monarchs migrating
with the wind

James A. Paulson
Narberth, Pennsylvania

honeycomb . . .
everything she can't
remember

Bill Pauly
Asbury, Iowa

white gulls against dark
and black in silhouette where
light is breaking through

Ellen Peckham
New York, New York

high desert
stillness
a beautiful nothingness

Patricia Pella
Woodland, California

carved and burned
grinning wooden bear statue
knots in stomach

Ann M. Penton
Green Valley, Arizona

sleepless night formatting loneliness

Stella Pierides
Neusaess, Bavaria, Germany

her cotton skirt
falls softly to the ground
steady rain

Greg Piko
Yass, New South Wales, Australia

sun tea
the rest of her
in that dress

Robert Piotrowski
Mississauga, Ontario, Canada

lost in yellow gold red leaves and found

Marian M. Poe
Plano, Texas

father's watch
the time it takes
to grow old

Robert Henry Poulin
Micco, Florida

latest poll
the butterfly
almost within reach

Perry L. Powell
College Park, Georgia

winter night
the everything
of a flame

Sandi Pray
St. Johns, Florida

the homeless man
hammers his tent stakes deeper
cold snap

Joan Prefontaine
Cottonwood, Arizona

test results pending the sway of palms

Sharon Pretti
San Francisco, California

becoming dusk—
leaves slowly fall
from the ancient oak

Patricia Prime
Auckland, New Zealand

Restringing my old mala—
one hundred six, one hundred seven—
Oh oh

> Richard M. Proctor
> Palm Springs, California

frost on the rails
graffiti scratched deep
into the carriage window

> Vanessa Proctor
> Sydney, New South Wales, Australia

courthouse wall—
O'Keeffe's flower
hangs crooked

> Andrew Punk
> Perrineville, New Jersey

evening on the lake—
oars dip into their own silence

David Rachlin
Stow, Massachusetts

the rising tides yield
fresh harvest of sand dollars
cold December morn

Barth H. Ragatz
Fort Wayne, Indiana

heavy flakes
sinking to earth
notes from a cello

Holli Rainwater
Fresno, Ohio

under the moon
waves rise and fall
our lives together

Ann Reardon
Sanibel, Florida

circling
the koi
rain drops

Michael Rehling
Presque Isle, Michigan

a dozen bruises
each one tender to the touch—
leftover apples

Joanne M. Reinbold
Wilmington, Delaware

metal hubcap
in a roadside ditch
a cloudy night

David H. Rembert, Jr.
Columbia, South Carolina

the wash line full
of sparrow song—
Easter Sunday

Bryan Rickert
Belleville, Illinois

winter burial
snow cushioning
my footsteps

Edward J. Rielly
Westbrook, Maine

crawling in traffic . . .
a cellist speeds through Stravinsky

Julie Riggott
Glendale, California

warmed with whiskey the winter moonlight

Joseph Robello
Novato, California

rain comes slow to learn my place

Chad Lee Robinson
Pierre, South Dakota

summer flash flood
my delicates' colors
run together

Jackie Maugh Robinson
Las Vegas, Nevada

letting go
of the steering wheel
a butterfly

Jim Rodriguez
Washougal, Washington

my mother's hair
scraped into a bun
piled leaves scrim-thin

Tess Romeis
Cedarburg, Wisconsin

fresh snow
the relief
of negative space

Michele Root-Bernstein
East Lansing, Michigan

Blue dragonfly—
what do you
listen to?

David Rosen
Eugene, Oregon

As the sun sets,
    the old fisherman sorts out
    the fish he can sell.

Sydell Rosenberg
United States

103

brittle brown seed pods
white envelopes in drawer
life awaits the thaw

Pamela Rosenblum
New York, New York

just the idea of it
full moon
behind these clouds

Ce Rosenow
Eugene, Oregon

breathless silence . . .
the moon is rising
over the Zuyderzee

Gabriel Rosenstock
Dublin, Ireland

a little bird
adds weight to the bough
almost spring . . .

> *Bruce Ross*
> *Hampden, Maine*

shunning sisters carve
rivulets of deep sorrow
desolate winds mourn

> *Roberta Rowland*
> *Campbell, California*

plum blossoms
lean over the wall
his wife's smile

> *Maggie Roycraft*
> *Morristown, New Jersey*

day by day
clouds, sky
sky, clouds

Lidia Rozmus
Vernon Hills, Illinois

traffic circle
night and I
revolve

Lyle Rumpel
Victoria, British Columbia, Canada

acorn . . .
the long silence
of falling

Patricia McKernon Runkle
Short Hills, New Jersey

monkey grass
leads me down the path
morning meditation

John Russo
Key West, Florida

x-ray over . . .
stuffed in the purse
my whitest bra

Margaret Rutley
Victoria, British Columbia, Canada

Old words
take on new life
—campfire

Melanie Sabol
Harwood, Maryland

the blur
where the bare rock
is the sun, too

Tom Sacramona
Plainville, Massachusetts

meteor shower
the time we think
we have

Michelle Schaefer
Bothell, Washington

Quinceañera day . . .
cream magnolias leak
a sweet fragrance

Judith Morrison Schallberger
San Jose, California

saguaro
the embrace
of a past lover

Mike Schoenburg
Skokie, Illinois

that special spark
in the waitress' eyes
catch of the day

Olivier Schopfer
Geneva, Switzerland

one of us
from a strange world
dragonfly

Ann K. Schwader
Westminster, Colorado

the sweetness
of silence
after the news

> Bill Sette
> Arlington, Virginia

Lifting others' souls
Our loneliness fades away
Cherish this approach

> Irfanulla Shariff
> South Elgin, Illinois

well worn kneeler
praying into the sound
of rain

> Adelaide B. Shaw
> Millbrook, New York

red wine fills my cup;
movies pour
    summer arrives.

Kendra Shaw
San Diego, California

morning ritual
with a splash my dreams
down the drain

Michael Sheffield
Kenwood, California

uchuva jamming with cumbia

Charles Shiotani
Watsonville, California

harpsichord pile-up
fingers still tangled
after Bach

Nancy Shires
Greenville, North Carolina

death rattle
small talk
during his wake

Gary Simpson
Fairview Heights, Illinois

autumn rains . . .
soaking in
edith piaf

D.W. Skrivseth
St. Anthony, Minnesota

lilac scent
all the things
he said

Olga Skvortsova
Saint Petersburg, Russia

tall silky grasses
caress the flowers
once she had long hair

Carole Slesnick
Bellingham, Washington

on the treadmill
going nowhere
again

Edna Small
Washington, DC

circle by circle . . .
a finch hops through
last night's rain

Michael Smeer
Hoofddorp NH, The Netherlands

walking in silence
after the funeral
footprints in the snow

Jackson D. Smith
Chicago, Illinois

Lessons long gone
As she cleans the erasers
Sunbeams sparkle

K.O. Smith
Asheville, North Carolina

lantern light
the river slips
through our fence

Barbara Snow
Eugene, Oregon

long summer—
my books
still on the thrift store shelf

Nicholas M. Sola
New Orleans, Louisiana

soft and pale
teneral dragonfly
a mother's worries

Sheila Sondik
Bellingham, Washington

forests catching fire
the blaze of sunrise
at its peak

Robert Sorrels
Brazil, Indiana

fireworks scraps eddy
against police barriers
gunpowder lingers

Michelle Spadafore
Brooklyn, New York

lightning flash—
raccoon's eyes reflect
astonishment

Robert Spice
Medford, New Jersey

mountains of money
relative strangers
circle the grave

Susan Squarey
Las Vegas, Nevada

Flowers on the fence
The first pink and gold trumpets.
Calling hummingbirds.

Carol Starr
Hudson, North Carolina

invisible wings
a flash of ruby
hummingbird

Toni Steele
Lomita, California

dragging a suitcase full of dirty clothes last night's moon

Bonnie Stepenoff
Chesterfield, Missouri

something lost
something forgotten
falling leaves

Christine Lamb Stern
Bayfield, Wisconsin

heirlooming

Jeff Stillman
Norwich, New York

ice fog
everything familiar
unfamiliar

Debbie Strange
Winnipeg, Manitoba, Canada

remembering
playground rules
he teases the girl he likes

Jim Sullivan
Glenview, Illinois

moonlighting crows in other colors

Alan Summers
Chippenham, Wiltshire, England

April Fools—
all of us on the bus
in our winter coats

Dean Summers
Seattle, Washington

Warm morning,
Shady porch,
Rocking chair.

Suzanne V. Surles
Jacksonville, North Carolina

The lark ascending
following
its own song

Dave Sutter
San Francisco, California

four leaf clover
between book pages—
forgotten desires

Polly W. Swafford
Kansas City, Missouri

spacetime curves around us
the light
skin tight

Lesley Anne Swanson
Coopersburg, Pennsylvania

coffin display
the various prices
of absence

George Swede
Toronto, Ontario, Canada

half a moon
    crickets
    in the good ear

                Rick Tarquinio
                Bridgeton, New Jersey

splattered raindrops
another nebulizer
treatment

        Frank J. Tassone
        Montebello, New York

        tradewinds
        half of the argument
        left for later

                Barbara Tate
                Winchester, Tennessee

promises only
daisies remember
wind blown clouds

Angela Terry
Lake Forest Park, Washington

strong coffee
luckily the color
of the rug

Maya Tettemer
Hereford, Pennsylvania

autumn leaves
the weight of parting
under pallbearers' feet

Padma Thampatty
Wexford, Pennsylvania

full moon
round every ant hole
a mound of silver wings

Jennifer Thiermann
Glenview, Illinois

the jay
using
his outdoor voice

Deanna Tiefenthal
Rochester, New York

learning a lost love
asked about me
autumn leaves swirling

Diane Tomczak
Shepherd, Michigan

a worn path
to the bridge
white clover

Mary Torregrossa
Baldwin Park, California

sumac   where the Redcoat fell

Charles Trumbull
Santa Fe, New Mexico

starry night—
adrift in the jazz band's
beautiful storm

Kevin Valentine
Mesquite, Texas

just hatched
the Luna Moth waits
for its wings to dry

Cor van den Heuvel
New York, New York

Seagull pivots left
Then turns right into the fog
Ocean buoy clangs

Barry Vitcov
Ashland, Oregon

A flash of lighting
Awakens the sleeping man
Standing on his porch

Tom Vorderer
Boston, Massachusetts

break of day
the mockingbird
his whole repertoire

Diane Wallihan
Port Townsend, Washington

morning mist . . .
a horse slips its nose
into the halter

Julie Warther
Dover, Ohio

haiku ~~group~~ workshop—
~~our~~ silly smiles queue~~ing~~ up
to ~~share scuttlebutt~~

Lew Watts
Santa Fe, New Mexico

lilac blossoms
nose pressed inside, inhaling
my grandmother

Mary Weidensaul
Granby, Massachusetts

staring at the kitchen wall
where the clock was

Linda Weir
Bowie, Maryland

first flurries . . .
a skateboard
broken in two

Michael Dylan Welch
Sammamish, Washington

tending wind chimes
gardening
in winter

Christine Wenk-Harrison
Lago Vista, Texas

house sparrow
an immigrant from Europe
just like me

Sharon R. Wesoky
Meadville, Pennsylvania

vacation—
we board out
the desert tortoise

Carmel Lively Westerman
Yuma, Arizona

riverfront
mosquitos
first kiss

Allyson Whipple
Austin, Texas

untrimmed palm
in the courtyard
folded umbrellas

Daniel White
Los Angeles, California

impending buds
yellow with caution
we cross the border

Scott Wiggerman
Albuquerque, New Mexico

distant motor
the light from the hill
turns inward

Ian Willey
Takamatsu, Kagawa, Japan

record drought   crows skim the plowlines

Billie Wilson
Juneau, Alaska

dewdrops
along the barbed wire
holding my breath!

Klaus-Dieter Wirth
Viersen, NRW, Germany

wavering heat
a crow lands
on a high tension wire

Robert Witmer
Tokyo, Japan

in moonlight
a spider web connects
the stars

Valorie Broadhurst Woerdehoff
Dubuque, Iowa

funeral
orchids stay to go home
with the living

James Won
Temple City, California

the wooded brook how i left the crowd

Steven Woodall
Tulsa, Oklahoma

moonlight
         softens the junkyard wrecks
                  . . . the sound of geese leaving

Keith Woodruff
Akron, Ohio

tiny box
all her wishes
twinkle

Theresa Woods
Canton, Ohio

whistling
within the observatory
autumn wind

Alison Woolpert
Santa Cruz, California

sleepless
through lace curtains a star
moves so slowly

Ruth Yarrow
Ithaca, New York

one hundred and two year old
cartoon animator
learning to fly with Dumbo

Sharon Yee
Torrance, California

sugar rush
feasting on the eye candy
of spring

Lori Zajkowski
New York, New York

ripe Brussels sprouts
some intended endearments
backfire

J. Zimmerman
Santa Cruz, California

every season
this pencil
upon my desk

- T56
Oakland, California

Publication Credits

Some of the poems in this anthology were first published in other media. The following information regarding previous publication has been provided by the authors.

Mimi Ahern - *Haiku 2015*, Modern Haiku Press (2015)

frances angela - *The Heron's Nest* XV:3 (2013)

Fay Aoyagi - *Frogpond* 38:2 (2015)

Susan B. Auld - *Chrysanthemum Dusk,* Red Moon Press (2016)

Ludmila Balabanova - *Modern Haiku* 40:3 (2009)

Francine Banwarth - Honorable Mention, Peggy Willis Lyles Haiku Award (2015)

Johnny Baranski - *The Heron's Nest* XVI:2 (2014)

Donna Bauerly - Shiki Monthly Kukai (February 2016)

Roberta Beary - *Presence* 53 (2015)

Ernest J. Berry - Honorable Mention, Lyrical Passion Contest (2010)

Robyn Hood Black - *A Hundred Gourds* 4:4 (2015)

Meik Blöttenberger - *A Hundred Gourds* 5:1 (2015)

brett brady - Akita International Haiku "Land of Poetry," 3rd Japan-Russia Haiku Contest (2015)

Susan Burch - *Grievous Angel* (2015)

Sean Carlton - *The Heron's Nest* XVI:1 (2014)

Terry Ann Carter - *Haiku Canada Broadsheet* (2016)

Tom Clausen - *Dim Sum,* Route 9 Haiku Group (2015)

Ellen Compton - *Frogpond* 38:3 (2015)

Susan Constable - *Modern Haiku* 46:2 (2015)

Bill Deegan - *A Hundred Gourds* 4:4 (2015)

Kristen Deming - *Presence* (2016)

Charlotte Digregorio - *Modern Haiku* 26:2 (1995)

Thomas Dougherty - *Frogpond* 37:3 (2014)

Tom Drescher - *The Heron's Nest* XVI:4 (2014)

Anna Eklund-Cheong - *Acorn* 35 (2015)

Marilyn Fleming - *Frogpond* 38:3 (2015)

Sylvia Forges-Ryan - *What Light There Is*, Red Moon
    Press (2016)
Mark Forrester - *bottle rockets* 17:1 (2015)
Susan Furst - *Poetry Super Highway*: Poet of the Week
    (December 14-20, 2015)
Ferris Gilli - *Modern Haiku* 46:3 (2015)
LeRoy Gorman - *Presence* 52 (2015)
David Grayson - Shiki Monthly Kukai (January 2009)
Anita Curran Guenin - *Southern California Haiku
    Study Group Anthology* (2011)
William Hart - *cloud eats mountain,* Red Moon Press
    (2013)
Michele L. Harvey - 3rd Place, Robert Spiess Memorial
    Haiku Awards (2016)
Barbara Hay - Featured on *NHK World Live,* with Alan
    Summers (September 2015)
Gary Hotham - *Frogpond* 38:3 (2015)
Jim Kacian - *NOON* 9
Elmedin Kadric - *The Heron's Nest* XVIII:1 (2016)
Barbara Kaufmann - *Acorn* 36 (2016)
Mary Kendall - *Failed Haiku - A Journal of English
    Senryu* (2016)
Bill Kenney - *Acorn* 36 (2016)
Deborah P Kolodji - *Rattle* (2015)
S.M. Kozubek - *Mayfly* 59 (2015)
Jill Lange - Shiki Monthly Kukai (March 2011)
Antoinette Libro - *The Haiku Calendar* (2015)
Bob Lucky - *Frogpond* 31:1 (2008)
E. Luke - *Above the Clouds, Yuki Teikei Haiku Society
    Members' Anthology* (2013);
*deep in the arroyo, Southern California Haiku
    Study Group Anthology* (2012)
Janis Albright Lukstein - *When Words Collide,
    SouthWest Manuscripters Anthology* (2014)
Patricia J. Machmiller - *The Heron's Nest* (2016)
Susan Godwin Madison - *Hummingbird* 26:1 (2016)
Ann Magyar - Runner-up, Golden Triangle Haiku
    Contest (2014)

Annette Makino - 2nd Place, Jane Reichhold
        International Prize, ukiaHaiku Festival
        (2016)
Anna Maris - *Under the Basho* (2015); Winner, *The*
        Haiku Calendar Competition (2016)
Jeannie Martin - *a circle of breath*, bottle rockets press
        (2016)
Thomas Martin - *Cattails* (2016)
Michael McClintock - *Clouds Peak* 2 (2006)
Vicki McCullough - *Haiku Canada Review* 7:2 (2013)
Robert B. McNeill - *Blithe Spirit* 26:2 (2016)
Connie R. Meester - *Modern Haiku* 30:1 (1999)
Walter Mehring - *Issa's Untidy Hut* (April 19, 2014)
Peter Meister - *Amelia* (1985)
Ben Moeller-Gaa - *Frozen Butterfly* 3 (2015)
Beverly Acuff Momoi - *Bones* 9 (2016)
Lenard D. Moore - *Right Hand Pointing* 95 (2016)
Ron C. Moss - *Whispers* (2015)
Marsh Muirhead - *Modern Haiku* 43:1 (2012)
Peter Newton - *The Heron's Nest* (2016)
Suzanne Niedzielska - *peach-hued,* rain puddle press
        (2014)
Patricia Noeth - *Lyrical Iowa* (2012)
Renée Owen - 3rd Place, HSA Henderson Haiku Contest
        (2015); *Frogpond* 39:2 (2016)
Roland Packer - *Haiku Canada Review* 9:2 (2015)
Tom Painting - *Acorn* 6 (2015)
Kathe L. Palka - *Modern Haiku* 46:2 (2015)
James A. Paulson - *Frogpond* 33:1 (2010)
Bill Pauly - The Betty Drevniok Award (2012); *Haiku*
        Canada Sheet (2012)
Ann M. Penton - *Wisconsin Poets' Calendar* (2014)
Stella Pierides - *Bones* 9
Greg Piko - *Presence* 53 (2015)
Sandi Pray - *The Heron's Nest* (2016)
Andrew Punk - *Frogpond* 38:3 (2015)
Ann Reardon - *Blue Ridge Haiku Journal* (2011)
Joseph Robello - *Acorn* 36 (2016)

Chad Lee Robinson - *Frozen Butterfly* 3 (2015)
Jackie Maugh Robinson - *Frogpond* 39:1 (2016)
Tess Romeis - *Hummingbird* 25:2 (2015)
David Rosen - *Spelunking Through Life* (2016)
Sydell Rosenberg - *American Haiku* 5:2 (1967); William
          J. Higginson, *The Haiku Handbook* (1985)
Michelle Schaefer - *Acorn* 36 (2016)
Mike Schoenburg - *A Hundred Gourds* 5:2 (2016)
Olivier Schopfer - *Prune Juice* 16 (2015)
Ann K. Schwader - *The Heron's Nest* XVI:4 (2014)
Irfanulla Shariff - *Poetrysoup.com* (June 18, 2015)
D.W. Skrivseth - *bottle rockets* 34 (2016)
Jackson D. Smith - *NeverEnding Story*
          - neverendingstoryhaikutanka.blogspot.com
Barbara Snow - *The Heron's Nest* (2009)
Christine Lamb Stern – *GEPPO* XXXIX:5 (2014); *The
          Plover and the Moonstone*, Yuki Teikei Haiku
          Society (2015)
Jeff Stillman - *Modern Haiku* 47:1 (2016)
Debbie Strange - 3rd Place, Shintai Haiku, *World Haiku
          Review* (January 2016)
Alan Summers - *Frogpond* 39:1 (2016)
Polly W. Swafford - *Thorny Locust* 12 (2004)
George Swede - *Frogpond* 38:3 (2015)
Rick Tarquinio - *Mostly Water* (2015)
Barbara Tate - *Modern Haiku* 47:2 (2016)
Diane Tomczak - *Modern Haiku* 47:2 (2016)
Kevin Valentine - *Chrysanthemum* 18 (2015)
Lew Watts - *Modern Haiku* 46:2 (2015)
Mary Weidensaul - *New England Letters* 64 (2016)
Scott Wiggerman - *Chrysanthemum* 17 (2015)
Valorie Broadhurst Woerdehoff - The Haiku Path,
          Holmes County Open Air Art Museum,
          Millersburg, Ohio.
Keith Woodruff - *bottle rockets* 34 (2016)
Alison Woolpert - *Modern Haiku* 47:1 (2016)
J. Zimmerman - *Frogpond* 38:1 (2015)

140

Index of Poets

brett brady
Chuck Brickley
Alan S. Bridges
Marjorie Buettner
Susan Burch
Merle Burgess
Alanna C. Burke
Norma Jean Byrkett
Cathy Cain
Cherry Campbell
Pris Campbell
Theresa A. Cancro
John J. Candelaria
Matthew Caretti
Sean Carlton
Eleanor Carolan
Terry Ann Carter
Thomas Chockley
Margaret Chula
Rick Clark
Tom Clausen
Lesley Clinton
Glenn G. Coats
Lysa Collins
Sue Colpitts
Ellen Compton
Susan Constable
Wanda Cook
Amelia Cotter
Dina E. Cox
Kyle D. Craig
Daniel Shank Cruz
Dan Curtis
John-Carl Davis
Pat Davis
Bill Deegan
Marcyn Del Clements
Kristen Deming

Brian DeMuth
Angelee Deodhar
Charlotte Digregorio
Connie Donleycott
Thomas Dougherty
Tom Drescher
Anna Eklund-Cheong
Art Elser
Haiku Elvis
Scott Endsley
Bruce England
Robert Epstein
Robert Ertman
Frances Farrell
Ignatius Fay
Bruce H. Feingold
Michael Fessler
Diarmuid Fitzgerald
Marilyn Fleming
Denise Fontaine-Pincince
Sylvia Forges-Ryan
Mark Forrester
Stanford M. Forrester
Robert Forsythe
Tom Lyon Freeland
Ida Freilinger
Terri L. French
Jay Friedenberg
Susan Furst
Marilyn Gabel
William Scott Galasso
Dianne Garcia
Tim Gardiner
Marita Gargiulo
Garry Gay
Ferris Gilli
Robert Gilliland
Joette Giorgis

Susan Godwin
Mel Goldberg
Kevin Goldstein-Jackson
John Gonzalez
Merrill Ann Gonzales
Brent Goodman
LeRoy Gorman
Mimi Gorman
Carolyn Noah Graetz
David Grayson
Mac Greene
Steven Greene
Ronald Grognet
Anita Curran Guenin
Maureen Lanagan Haggerty
Autumn Noelle Hall
John J. Han
Bryan Hansel
Tim Happel
Patty Hardin
Jon Hare
William Hart
Michele L. Harvey
Patricia Harvey
Arch Haslett
Tomoko Hata
Barbara Hay
Elizabeth Hazen
Cynthia Henderson
Randall Herman
Christopher Herold
Poppy Herrin
Merle D. Hinchee
Carolyn M. Hinderliter
Judith Hishikawa
Ruth Holzer
Gary Hotham
Elizabeth Howard

Marshall Hryciuk
Marilyn Humbert
David Jacobs
Eric Jennings
Jeanne Jorgensen
Jim Kacian
Elmedin Kadric
Barbara Kaufmann
Robert K. Keim
Julie Bloss Kelsey
Mary Kendall
Maggie Kennedy
Phillip Kennedy
Bill Kenney
Howard Lee Kilby
Mary Kipps
kjmunro
Marylouise Knight
Tricia Knoll
Dianne Koch
Deb Koen
Deborah P Kolodji
Ed Kosiewicz
S.M. Kozubek
Henry W. Kreuter
Steve Kuntz
Ron LaMarsh
Jill Lange
David G. Lanoue
Jim Laurila
Michael Henry Lee
Phyllis Lee
Brenda Lempp
Antoinette Libro
Bruce Linton
Joseph Llewellyn
Cyndi Lloyd
Renee Londner

Gregory Longenecker
Amy Losak
Bob Lucky
E. Luke
Janis Albright Lukstein
Doris Lynch
Patricia J. Machmiller
Carole MacRury
Ann Magyar
Annette Makino
C.R. Manley
Anna Maris
Jeannie Martin
Thomas Martin
Michael McClintock
Wilma McCracken
Vicki McCullough
Tanya McDonald
Joe McKeon
Dorothy McLaughlin
Robert B. McNeill
Connie R. Meester
Walter Mehring
Peter Meister
RaNae Merrill
Ben Moeller-Gaa
Matthew Moffett
Beverly Acuff Momoi
Mike Montreuil
Lenard D. Moore
Ron C. Moss
Marsh Muirhead
Leanne Mumford
Marie Louise Munro
Sandra J. Nantais
Peter Newton
Suzanne Niedzielska
Patti Niehoff

Mike Nierste
Nika
Patricia Noeth
Nola Obee
Frank O'Brien
Karen O'Leary
Ellen Grace Olinger
Bob Oliveira
Ken Olson
Marian Olson
Mark Alan Osterhaus
Renée Owen
Roland Packer
Tom Painting
Kathe L. Palka
Carol Ann Palomba
Trilla Pando
Sarah Paris
Sarah Patterson
Thomas W. Paul
James A. Paulson
Bill Pauly
Ellen Peckham
Patricia Pella
Ann M. Penton
Stella Pierides
Greg Piko
Robert Piotrowski
Marian M. Poe
Robert Henry Poulin
Perry L. Powell
Sandi Pray
Joan Prefontaine
Sharon Pretti
Patricia Prime
Richard M. Proctor
Vanessa Proctor
Andrew Punk

David Rachlin
Barth H. Ragatz
Holli Rainwater
Ann Reardon
Michael Rehling
Joanne M. Reinbold
David H. Rembert, Jr.
Bryan Rickert
Edward J. Rielly
Julie Riggott
Joseph Robello
Chad Lee Robinson
Jackie Maugh Robinson
Jim Rodriguez
Tess Romeis
Michele Root-Bernstein
David Rosen
Sydell Rosenberg
Pamela Rosenblum
Ce Rosenow
Gabriel Rosenstock
Bruce Ross
Roberta Rowland
Maggie Roycraft
Lidia Rozmus
Lyle Rumpel
Patricia McKernon Runkle
John Russo
Margaret Rutley
Melanie Sabol
Tom Sacramona
Michelle Schaefer
Judith Morrison Schallberger
Mike Schoenburg
Olivier Schopfer
Ann K. Schwader
Bill Sette
Irfanulla Shariff

Adelaide B. Shaw
Kendra Shaw
Michael Sheffield
Charles Shiotani
Nancy Shires
Gary Simpson
D.W. Skrivseth
Olga Skvortsova
Carole Slesnick
Edna Small
Michael Smeer
Jackson D. Smith
K.O. Smith
Barbara Snow
Nicholas M. Sola
Sheila Sondik
Robert Sorrels
Michelle Spadafore
Robert Spice
Susan Squarey
Carol Starr
Toni Steele
Bonnie Stepenoff
Christine Lamb Stern
Jeff Stillman
Debbie Strange
Jim Sullivan
Alan Summers
Dean Summers
Suzanne V. Surles
Dave Sutter
Polly W. Swafford
Lesley Anne Swanson
George Swede
Rick Tarquinio
Frank J. Tassone
Barbara Tate
Angela Terry

Maya Tettemer
Padma Thampatty
Jennifer Thiermann
Deanna Tiefenthal
Diane Tomczak
Mary Torregrossa
Charles Trumbull
Kevin Valentine
Cor van den Heuvel
Barry Vitcov
Tom Vorderer
Diane Wallihan
Julie Warther
Lew Watts
Mary Weidensaul
Linda Weir
Michael Dylan Welch
Christine Wenk-Harrison
Sharon R. Wesoky
Carmel Lively Westerman
Allyson Whipple
Daniel White
Scott Wiggerman
Ian Willey
Billie Wilson
Klaus-Dieter Wirth
Robert Witmer
Valorie Broadhurst Woerdehoff
James Won
Steven Woodall
Keith Woodruff
Theresa Woods
Alison Woolpert
Ruth Yarrow
Sharon Yee
Lori Zajkowski
J. Zimmerman
- T56